Whole Learning: *Whole Child*

by Joy Cowley

TWG

A Professional Resource Book from
The Wright Group • Bothell, WA

Whole Learning: Whole Child

©1994 by Joy Cowley
©1994 Wright Group Publishing, Inc.

The Wright Group
19201 120th Avenue NE
Bothell, WA 98011-9512

Printed in the United States of America

10 9 8 7 6 5 4 3

ISBN: 0-7802-1484-6

This book is dedicated with affection and gratitude to American kindergarten and elementary school teachers. They are the "sheroes" and heroes of a nation and the hope for the future of the world.

Contents

Introduction

There is nothing in this book that you don't already know. We have all been children and we all recognize the truths of childhood when someone or something reminds us of them. I need to be constantly reminded. I work with children every day, directly or indirectly, but I can still lose sight of my personal experience of childhood. I hear this little voice in me saying that childhood is something I've put behind me, and without realizing it, I can project that attitude onto children. I can easily and unintentionally begin to talk about children as objects of educational programs, seeing them as students and adults as teachers, although I know that this is a two-way dynamic with children also being teachers and adults, students.

It is as a student that I have written this book, learning from teachers, listening to children, making observations and discoveries in the classroom while also trying to keep in touch with the child within me. As I traveled throughout America visiting classrooms, many educators have asked me to put my thoughts about teaching and learning on paper. This book was put together in response to requests from American teachers who have been discovering the freedom and success of whole learning in the classroom. I am grateful to those teachers for their affirmation, their enthusiasm, and above all, for the great things they are doing for the children in their classes. But I *do* find a problem in answering their requests. Whole learning is, by its very nature, a seamless whole. Attempting to define it in linear fashion, chapter by chapter, is a bit like taking a circle, straightening it out, and segmenting it, while still referring to it as a circle. I have tried to overcome this difficulty by laying a metaphorical grid over the circle in order to deal with various aspects of whole learning. There is some repetition due to overlap in some of the chapters, but this is inevitable. I hope you benefit in some way from my insights into children from my point of view as a children's book writer. And thank you for your commitment to the child's world.

**Chapter One**

Beginnings

I have never been a teacher. What I know about the teaching of reading comes from my own early reading experience, from that of my children, from the thousands of children I've worked with, and from the teachers who have so generously made their expertise and their students available to me. I have worked directly with early reading students in the United States of America, Canada, Australia, Singapore, Fiji, the Cook Islands, Brunei, and New Zealand.

My own introduction to reading was not a very happy one. Indeed, it was so difficult that it still influences everything I write for children. This is how I remember it:

I came to school at a later age than usual and with no preschool experience or knowledge about books. This was partly because both my parents suffered ill health and were on a social welfare benefit, and also due to the attitude still alive then that education was not a priority for girls. I was eight before I owned my first book, but when I began school I was already being taught to cook, knit, sew, and crochet. These skills were considered the most important part of a girl's learning.

There came a day when I found myself in a crowded classroom with children younger than I, who could all make at least some sense of the black squiggles on white paper that were hung on the easel before us. I couldn't. These squiggles were not pictures and had no recognizable shape. I could find no clue to their meaning. All I could do was guess, and when my guess was wrong the teacher hit my legs with a ruler.

I quickly adapted to other classroom activities— drawing, making clay models, cutting colored paper, and threading beads. I found for the first time the pleasure of having friends. But I can still remember the cold fear that possessed me when the teacher called us to the reading groups: "Bring up your books and stand in line."

Because I can't remember actually breaking through to reading, I don't know how that struggle was resolved. The next vivid memory comes from a different class in a different school. The teacher was handing out some "real" books. These were not "reading" books with lists of words and sounds. They had wonderful stories with pictures on every page, and I was given one of them. It was the story of a duckling called *Ping* (*The Story about Ping* by Marjorie Flack, with illustrations by Kurt Wiese), and I read it, my first real book, from cover to cover. I was so excited by the story that I forgot that I wasn't a good reader. I became lost on the Yangtze River, far away from the classroom and my fear of printed words. The cover of that book was a door to another world and I had joyfully entered, meeting my own expectation that I would find excitement and adventure. I didn't want to come back to the classroom. When the story ended, I promptly returned to the first page and began again, making a new discovery. The story was exactly the same with the second reading! It hadn't changed as spoken stories did. I had discovered the constancy of print.

It seemed to me that after *Ping* everything changed, and I instantly became an avid and accomplished reader. I know it didn't happen like that. The instant change was in my attitude. Reading was no longer an exercise without meaning. It allowed me to gain access into stories, fanciful and wonderful stories. As often as I picked up a book, I could journey to other worlds and have safe adventures.

My appetite for the written word and my fascination with it became limitless. When I was nine, my father took me to join the local library. The children's section was very small, but a wise librarian guided my rapacious appetite to certain authors in the adult section: Dumas, Verne, Hugo, the Brontës, Dickens, Cooper, Twain, Melville, Stevenson. My parents, who had initially been pleased at my progress, were now alarmed, fearing that so much reading would make me "soft in the head." There were restrictions on reading at home that necessitated a flashlight under the bedcovers at night, and at school I developed a split focus—absorbing the book in my lap under the desk with my eyes, while my ears remained alert for the teacher's questions.

In my twelfth year a kindly neighbor gave me an old bicycle, and I rode to school with a book opened and propped on the handlebars. One morning, somewhere amidst an exciting story, I pedaled into the back of a parked van. The bike and I both suffered some surface damage, but that was not the end of the matter. The law became involved, and at a general school assembly I appeared between the principal and a traffic officer as an example of irresponsible road behavior.

About this time, the enthusiam I had gained for stories from reading countless adventures written by gifted writers began to appear in my own writing. With the encouragement of a teacher who valued creativity, stories began to flow. I "published" comic strips for the kids in the neighborhood, told and wrote long serials for my sisters, and had poems and stories published on the children's page of a Wellington newspaper.

As a high school student, I had to work part-time to bring extra income to the family. I had a variety of jobs, but the best was in my last year at school when I worked for three hours every afternoon as the editor of the "News for Children" page of the local newspaper. I was offered full employment with the paper as a cadet reporter, but my parents had other ideas; they apprenticed me to the local pharmacist. Four years later, I married and in the next five years had two daughters and two sons.

As in the United States, the 1960s was a time of great social change in New Zealand. Teenagers were finding their own identity and a culture based on their music; there were new migrant populations from the islands of the South Pacific, each nation bringing its own language and the riches of its traditions; the country's colonial ties with Britain were being loosened; television was introduced into homes; and there was a remarkable flowering of children's books, especially in the picture book genre. As all these influences reached the classroom, educational concepts changed. Sylvia Ashton-Warner was a strong voice of the 1960s, but there were many other teachers like her who were rethinking the traditional methods of teaching and moving toward a child-centered approach to learning.

In the 1960s, I was involved with my young family and our farm, writing short stories and then novels for an adult audience in my spare time. My novels were published in America and England, and my only children's stories were bedtime sagas invented for my children. Then I realized that my second child, Edward, had a reading problem. His background was different from mine. Edward loved books. His own shelves were well-stocked, and every Friday there was a family excursion to the public library. But Edward didn't relate to fantasy. Stories had to be factual. He collected books on deep-sea diving, aircraft, mechanical diggers, trains, shipwrecks, sports cars, and dinosaurs. He listened to the texts as we read them, memorized facts and figures, and believed that when he started school he would be able to read these books for himself. That didn't happen. His two sisters were reading and Edward was concerned. Why hadn't this happened for him?

Edward's teacher was an intelligent, loving woman

who talked freely about the problems she had with the standard reading texts—dull little books, poorly illustrated and poorly produced. They were adequate for children like my daughters who were going to read anyway, but not for Edward and children like him in the school. They were, as Edward repeatedly told me, boring. They held no meaning for him.

With his teacher's help, I wrote material for Edward. They were simple graded stories about him and his interests, illustrated with drawings or pictures cut from magazines. I saw in him the change I had experienced years before when I encountered *Ping*. Edward forgot that he was doing "boring old reading" and became involved in a story that interested him. I then worked with other children in his class, moving on to students in other schools. Some of these children had been arbitrarily labeled dyslexic. Others were described as having social/emotional problems. This may have been true. But as I observed them, I realized that whatever the supposed difficulty, it didn't seem to affect those activities that interested the children. They had good mobility, coordination, and problem-solving skills when playing ball games, working with building sets, assembling train sets, doing puzzles, and picking up tunes and rhythms on musical instruments. The problems seemed to exist only with reading. All, without exception, adopted a defensive body posture when they were given a school reading book to work with. They described reading as "hard" or "boring" and used negative language to describe themselves as readers. As I wrote for and worked with these children, it became apparent that much of the problem lay with adult-centered educational methods and books that had no meaning for them. I learned, too, that the stories I wrote needed to be affirming of the child to make the child feel good about herself. They needed to be exciting stories with a strong story shape—beginning, middle, and ending. A surprise ending was a reward to those who read the entire story. But the most valuable tool of all was humor. Whether the story was fact or fantasy, humor was always a great plus. Jokes quickly thawed a frozen attitude to reading. No one could laugh and be tense at the same time.

In the late 1960s and 1970s, I wrote for the New Zealand Education Department's *School Journals*, and also for teacher friends who made "blown-up" books from some of the stories. These were the forerunners of the big shared reading books as we know them. The text was hand-lettered on doubled sheets of brown paper, and illustrations were done by teachers or students. The books were used for shared reading, and there was pressure from teachers to have them published. But where?

In the late 1970s, the New Zealand Education Department planned an extensive revision of the existing reading program and planned to add new material. They conducted a series of workshops to train established authors, of whom I was one. The training was intensive and thorough, and I learned much about the mechanics of text production and illustration. I wrote a lot of stories for the new series but then learned that it would be five years before the first books could be published. The teachers I worked with said they couldn't wait that long. The need was desperate.

One morning in 1979, after a conversation with a group of teachers, I phoned my friend June Melser and asked her if she would be interested in creating a reading program with me. June was a retired teacher, college of education lecturer, *School Journal* editor, and an educator in the Sylvia Ashton-Warner mold. She initially refused but later accepted, and we began work on a graded reading program we called STORY BOX®.

June and I had our own dreams for STORY BOX. It would be different from any reading program previously published. From the first levels, it would have real stories, illustrated and produced with the quality of trade picture books. The stories would be child-centered, exciting, affirming, supportive of the child as reader and person. We wanted to create a program that would make all children winners.

For the next five years, STORY BOX was not just a job, it was a way of living. It consumed us. June did most of the grading and editing of my stories, adding her own collections of retold traditional tales. With her awareness of the child's print requirements, she also commanded the pagination of the books, the print size, shape and placement. I worked on the picture side. This involved visiting art and design schools to look for new illustrators, visualizing the books for early reading, and writing illustration briefs, doing rough sketches in the books sent to teachers who took part in classroom trials.

That was the beginning. The rest of the story

involves a New Zealand publisher, Wendy Pye, who was then working for Shortland Publications, and her association with the innovative American educational publishers The Wright Group. It was The Wright Group who gave the STORY BOX reading program its American identity.

June Melser has retired. For me it is an ongoing story. I continue to write for Wendy Pye, who now publishes the SUNSHINE™ books distributed to U.S. schools by The Wright Group. I also write stories directly for The Wright Group. Personal development is also a part of my story, as I learn from an ever-increasing number of teachers and children throughout the world.

Chapter Two

The World of Story

We are a story-making people. We communicate through stories. We become visible to ourselves through stories. Our memories come back to us in story form, and when we plan for the future, we often design stories about where we would like to be years from now. Every human achievement, every scientific discovery has its origins in story. Let's think about that for a moment. Can we name any invention or discovery that hasn't been anticipated in advance by the human mind?

Whenever a group of people comes together, we have story. This happens especially when people gather with members of their own sex. Waiting at the bus stop or the grocery store, over dinner or morning coffee, there it is—story. "Guess what happened yesterday?" "Have you seen this morning's paper?" "I was talking to him and he reckons..." "When I was your age..." Story fills all the spaces in our daily activity.

By story, I don't mean works of creative imagination,

although they are a part of life's story. I am referring to the way we document our lives. For all of us, story is the binding material of community. It carries our history and our cultural lineage. It is the vehicle for our identity and the natural way we project ourselves and our ideas. By exchanging stories with each other, we expand our knowledge and grow personally.

For the purpose of definition, we can say there are two kinds of story, the conscious and the unconscious, and the two mingle. Simplistically, the conscious reveals what we know by rational means; and the unconscious reveals that that we intuitively recognize but do not intellectually process.

Conscious story is what we might call factual story—history or "her" story. It is information about ourselves and our environment that we pass on to others. The unconscious represents that uncharted area of the self which is revealed in dreams and in the imaginative work we call art. In writing, unconscious story will wear a factual disguise, and this we call fiction. Now, some of us tend to put fact and fiction in widely separate categories, but they are both part of the same iceberg—one above the surface, the other below, hidden and viewed only by indirect means.

When student writers talk about fiction as though it were something magical plucked from the air, I point out that the "made-up" story is not so much invention as discovery, an uncovering of things already there. We don't make stories up out of nothing. When we "create" fiction, we take experience and put it into a new arrangement, one that expresses for us some truth that

cannot be described in a factual way. The fiction writer
is a bit like a cook drawing on a variety of common
ingredients, mixing and cooking them in the mystery of
her own unconscious experience to make a new dish.

To a certain extent the same is true of what we call
nonfiction or factual writing. There is no such thing as
truly objective reporting. The historian, the journalist,
the recorder of information will reveal much of herself
in the type of story she tells, how she tells it, the data
selected, and the language used. We observe that it is
the mature and centered writer who will give a mature
and balanced factual report. This is something we
should remember when we are watching TV news
broadcasts and documentaries. We are seeing what
some person wants us to see. We are getting information mixed with a personal bias.

So really, while the terms fact and fiction might be
useful when looking for books in a library, they become
blurred when we look at story and the story-making
process. As children we were taught that fact is true
and fiction is untrue. As adults we know the fiction of
fact and the truth of fiction.

The written word is the most recent vehicle for story.
We have a number of ancient ways of storytelling:
speech, picture, music, dance, signals, acting, and mime.
Nearly every five-year-old child beginning school has
experienced at least one of these and is receptive to oral,
physical, and pictorial communication. Written language, however, is often new territory for the child. For
children who have not had preschool experiences with
books, print can also be very daunting territory. Both

the word symbols themselves and their purposes are unfamiliar to them.

Some children come to school with a limited and perhaps negative experience of oral language. For children who have had consistent verbal abuse, there is absolutely no connection between language as they know it and the books they encounter at school.

We know that most children come to school as eager explorers. My concern as a writer of early reading material is not with the child who has a keen appetite for books and reading. He's going to read anyway, and there will always be plenty of reading material available to him. I am concerned with producing books for the child who approaches reading with an indifferent or tense or even fearful attitude.

What kind of material appeals to children? Their own stories, and more often than not a story that wears the guise of fantasy. In the first chapter, I mentioned my own breakthrough with the book *Ping*, the story of a little duckling who lives on a houseboat on the Yangtze River. Why does this story have such strong appeal for children of different generations and cultures? Because it's not really about a duckling but a child. And what's the worst thing that can happen to a young child? To get lost, to suddenly discover that she is alone, all security gone. Ping the duckling is lost and then found—strong drama, happy ending. The young reader can experience the trauma in the safety of a book and then solve Ping's problems by reading to the last page of the happy ending.

What about the story of *Mrs. Wishy-washy*? It's a

simple tale of farm animals who joyfully rush back to the mud after being scrubbed by Mrs. Wishy-washy. It also describes rebellion against that particular form of adult authority that puts more value on tubbing and scrubbing than on having fun.

We know that Beatrix Potter's Peter Rabbit is a child, not a rabbit. When we examine the subtext we realize that the social and emotional age of Peter Rabbit corresponds neatly with that of his most enthusiastic young readers.

Dr. Seuss's *Green Eggs and Ham* is much loved by children everywhere but held in reservation by some adults. Why? I suspect that it's because many adults have forgotten what it's like to be presented with a new food and told, "Eat it! It's good for you!" As we look at stories that appeal to children, we should also be aware that many children's books are actually written for adults. These are the books that you and I cherish. We buy them, collect them, and give them to our friends, and we often wonder why children don't appreciate them as much as we do. This is because the books are written from an adult point of view, embracing adult values, adult humor, and adult resolutions to adult problems. They don't necessarily appeal to children.

Censorship of children's books has always been in the hands of adults and often without reference to children and their needs. Some censorship is necessary, of course. No one would expose a young tree to the elements: it needs careful staking and shelter. But at the same time we must make sure that our support for the plant does not restrict its growth. So it is with children.

The guidance we give them should be consistent with their needs and sensibilities, not ours. An example of the way we apply censorship from our own anxieties is seen in our insistence on removing anything remotely suggestive of violence from children's literature. The more horrific the violence in the world around us, the greater our insistence that we present to our children another world of sweetness and light.

Of course, strong violence is unacceptable and should be censored. In their reading, children should always be given options to violent confrontation—in other words, be offered tools that will help them cope with life. When children's books suggest that people never get angry, never shout and bully, and are never unkind or unjust, they are removed from the child's experience of the world. At best, the child will not relate to the book. At worst, such a book can alienate the child and make her feel that she is alone in her personal experience of violence.

Some years ago, I wrote a story called "Fighting Friday" for one of the New Zealand Department of Education's *School Journals*. It concerned an argument between parents as witnessed by children and the children's fears when the argument escalated to a total breakdown in communication. This story, the first of its kind in the *School Journal*, evoked classroom discussion on a national scale. It was revealed that almost every child believed that his or her parents were the only mom and dad in the world who argued. The expansion of awareness and relief was most therapeutic, especially for those young people who were feeling responsible for parental discord.

I will deal fully with child-centered story in the next chapter. Let's now look at five key functions that stories should serve for young readers.

1. **Entertainment.** The story has high interest value and is a real story with a satisfying ending.
2. **Affirmation.** The story portrays the child as a winner, a problem solver, and an authority. It does not treat the child as a novice.
3. **Intimacy.** The story meets the child on a one-to-one basis with a personal message of love and understanding.
4. **Extension.** The story extends the child's awareness of himself and his environment.
5. **Empowerment.** The story becomes a resource for the child's personal development and creativity.

Chapter Three

The Healing Power of Words

*A*s story-making people, we are aware of the power of language. Words shape our society. We use their potency in politics, courtrooms, classrooms, advertising, and in influencing people and events. We could say that we live in an age not so much of "mass communication" as "mass over-communication." We tend to become desensitized and closed-minded. Most of this volley of verbiage is quickly judged and set aside. As mature individuals, we have the experience necessary for the development of communication skills. We know how to evaluate language aimed at us, but all the same, we are well aware of what words can do to our self-esteem when they are fired at us in a personal way.

Now, what about those people who don't have the experience of life and communication to evaluate language, those who are vulnerable to the violence of words? By people, I mean young children. And by violence, I'm not talking about graphic description of physical violence. I mean the emotional violence done when language is used to induce guilt or feelings of failure, when it makes a small person a prisoner of her or his smallness.

There are times when we are all guilty of using language this way. Sometimes we don't know the far-reaching effect of a few hastily spoken words. A nine-year-old girl, feeling that her mother didn't love her, sobbed, "I wish I had never been born!" The mother, frustrated beyond patience, fired back, "So do I!" Forty years later a woman still carried within her a nine-year-old girl who was sobbing and hurting from the wound of those three careless words.

On the other hand, words can have great healing power. They can gather together the fragments of a life and make them whole. Words can love spontaneity back into a child, rebuild self-esteem. Words can say openly or covertly, "You are a beautiful and special person. Don't you think you're wonderful? I do!"

When I was young, the popular view was that too much praise was bad for a child. It was supposed to make a child arrogant, conceited, competitive, and so on. But a child cannot be praised too much. The pushy, demanding child is displaying a hunger for affirmation. Satisfy that hunger and the egocentric behavior will curl up and go to sleep like a contented cat.

What about the five-year-old ready to start school? The child is starting to interact with the language in her first reading books. This five-year-old belongs to a society that is competitive rather than cooperative. Most of us nurture the ideal of a cooperative society, but it's not the reality. Homo sapiens follow the laws of nature, which are competitive rather than compassionate, in a game of life that emphasizes the importance of winning. For every winner, there are a number of losers, and if you're small and powerless, you know a lot about losing. The five-year-old starting school is already well experienced in defeat, which is why it is so important that her first interactions with text provide success and empowerment.

Let us consider the ways in which a small child knows defeat. There is adult authority, which so often renders the child helpless. Sometimes this is necessary. In areas where the child's welfare is at stake, adults have to occasionally work on the "might is right" principle. But well-intentioned adults can play manipulative games with young children.

I was once invited to a meal with a young family. The parents seemed determined to impress me with the good behavior of their children, but they were faced with mutiny by their three-year-old son, who was refusing to eat his vegetables. The scenario went like this:

> Father: "You can't have your dessert until you've finished your vegetables."
> Son: "Don't like it!"
> Father (taking off his watch and placing it on the table between them): "I'm giving you one minute to eat your vegetables. If you don't, I'm going to have your dessert."
> (Son begins to cry loudly.)

Father: "...forty, thirty-nine, thirty-eight..."

Son: "Wa-a-ah! Not going to! I hate it! Wa-a-ah!"

Father: "...four, three, two, one. All right. You can't
   say I didn't warn you." (Father eats the dessert.)

Son (becoming frenzied, jumping out of his chair and
   hitting his father): "I'm going to get a scissors and
   cut you in half! I'm going to bomb you to bits!"
(Father picks up son, spanks him, and puts him in
the bedroom. Father comes back to the table.)

Father (to me): "That's the influence of television for
   you."

Children may have parents who meet all the ideals of
parenthood, but there is still the world out there that
denies children authority, seeing them in terms of adult
investment. Children are keen to sense when they are
not valued for themselves. Adult love and guidance is
one thing, adult control and dictatorship another. All
children, to some extent, will come in contact with
adults who project their own childhood frustrations
upon them. It is a self-repeating pattern over the
generations.

Being small in a big world is difficult in other ways,
too. There is the problem of being physically too small,
of not being able to reach things, move things, lift
things. It's not being able to see in a theater, being
surrounded by a forest of legs in a crowd, being at the
mercy of adults who feel they have the right to pick you
up, squeeze you, tickle you until you can't breathe.
Then there is the problem of lack of skills. Being small
is putting on gloves and having two glove fingers left
over. It's a knot in shoelaces and buttons that don't

match buttonholes and zippers that won't do up. It's not understanding the relative size of things and being scared of the possibility of being sucked up the vacuum cleaner or drawn down the bath or shower drain. It's the ordeal of getting off the top of the escalator. It's the fear of the violent energy of dreams and the monsters that inhabit areas of ignorance.

I am not referring to the underprivileged child, one who has been abused in some way, but to all young children. All, to some degree, know powerlessness.

Fortunately, most children are very resilient. We went through the same processes ourselves, and most of us learned to bounce back. Difficulties became challenges that, when overcome, helped us to develop problem-solving skills. But when a young child has had too much defeat in her life, she becomes a walled fortress. She retreats from further risk. She will not try anything new that carries a chance of failure, and we have that child coming to reading with an attitude of defeat already entrenched within her.

With this awareness as our starting point, let us look again at the five ways in which a story can be a gift to the young reader. I will take the list given at the end of chapter 2 and examine each more fully, relating it to our individual experience of books and children in the classroom.

1. Entertainment

The story should be a *real* story with high interest value and a satisfying ending. Children need stories that come from their world, not from some adult view of

what that world should be. Much material is written
from the ideals that adults have for children, rather than
from the realities of the child's experience. Children
read for meaning. If a story doesn't truthfully reflect
their feelings and experience of life, they will not relate
to it. To those writers who tend to use patronizing
language in their manuscripts for children, I have
suggested the following: Write for children as you
would write for adults, but stay within their experience
of life and language.

Children's books should be of high interest, with
entertaining stories supported by quality illustrations.
There should be meticulous production standards, with
care given to every detail of text and illustration layout
so the reader doesn't have to struggle for meaning. We
should remember that we do not read dull and difficult
books by choice. Why should we expect that of our
children?

The young child brings to reading three special gifts
that few adults have. The first gift is a ready sense of
wonder; the child is quick to see new experience as
fresh and enchanting. The second gift is a sense of the
ridiculous; the child looks for jokes and finds them. The
third gift is a feeling for the quirkiness of words.
Rhyme, rhythm, alliteration, puns, nonsense language,
and animal sounds are all appetizing to the early reader.
Children are keen to explore all the fun that language
has to offer. In acknowledging these gifts and using
them, we can greatly assist the child's language development.

Children understand that a *real* story has a simple

story shape: beginning, middle, and end. The end is important. It needs to be positive and satisfying. Flat or open-ended conclusions might be all right for older readers, but they leave the young child with the feeling that the last pages of the story have been ripped out.

2. Affirmation

The story should portray the child as winner, problem solver, and authority. It should not treat the child as a novice.

Many children come to school expecting to read. There is something about school that is the "open sesame" to reading. The child believes that reading will happen automatically, and it is important that this expectation be met. The child should be able to go to school and on the first day, pick up a *real* book with a *real* story and "read" it for meaning. This means that children need access to a variety of books that are very simple. They should have repetitive, one-line text in which most of the story unfolds in the picture sequence. (Children of the video age are very adept at picking up pictorial story development.) But this is not to say that these are simply picture books. The child is also becoming familiar with a carefully graded text. Most important, the child sees herself as a reader. It doesn't matter that she is still a long way from being a fluent reader. She knows she can "read" a whole book from beginning to end. In her own eyes, she is a reader and what she believes will become reality.

While the book affirms the child's expectations of himself as a reader, it also affirms him as a person in its

subject matter. Have you noticed how children will
always identify with the smallest character in a book? If
the story is about an adult and a child, they will, of
course, identify with the child. If it's about a child and
a mouse, they will identify with the mouse. In child-
centered story, small is beautiful and valuable. Small is
clever, small can do anything. Small is always the
winner.

3. Intimacy

The story should meet the child on a one-on-one basis
with a personal message of love and understanding.

As adults, we are anxious to do the best for our
children. We spend a lot of time trying to train young
people to be responsible adults and, in all sorts of subtle
or not-so-subtle ways, we place burdens of social
responsibility on small shoulders. We write stories
about children who are kind and understanding, who
are unselfish, who are givers and forgivers, who are
helpful and creative—children who make great sacri-
fices for other people. This is all OK, but we tend to try
to put up the building without first laying foundations.
Altruism is a natural overflowing of self-love and self-
esteem. Social responsibility comes out of responsibility
for self, and that in turn comes out of self-respect and
self-confidence. Social messages in literature are good,
but first and foremost, stories should love the young
reader. An early reading book should be love-based; it
should be for the child on an intimate one-to-one level
appropriate for that child's stage of development. It
should make the child feel good about himself. It

should do something to redress the balance between the powerful and the powerless.

4. Extension

The story should extend the child's awareness of himself and his environment.

While dealing with the familiar, the story should also offer the new, especially supporting the child's need to make meaning of her world. In this way, it should gradually extend the child's language experience by introducing new ideas, always in the context of meaning. The child soon learns that books provide safe entry into other worlds where the reader has authority as explorer and discoverer, and the more she reads, the more she is able to read.

5. Empowerment

The story should become a resource for the child's personal development and creativity.

The early reading book should support and affirm the child in all the ways mentioned, helping the child to cope with difficulties and to see himself as important. It should also be open to innovation and provide a launching pad for the child's own creativity. The young child is not yet able to write a creative work from his own language experience without a model. The text of the book can provide a structure upon which he can hang his own words and pictures. Thus, young children see themselves not just as readers, but also as authors and illustrators.

Chapter Four

A Little About Learning

*T*he last decade of the twentieth century has brought sophisticated technology to the study of brain functioning. Previously, we could study only the unconscious brain, and conscious activity remained hidden. Now, with microchip engineering, we have instruments that can track conscious brain activity through blood flow and fine changes in magnetic fields. Brain action and reaction can be accurately measured and recorded. This sudden expansion of research has given us a library of scientific data that reinforces everything we already know about natural or holistic learning.

When we use natural learning methods in early reading, we label them the following: "integrated learning," "whole language," or "child-centered learning." In New Zealand schools where there are no alternative learning systems (basal or phonic), the approach to learning to read has no label. It is simply the way all children in the country learn in their early years at school. The problem with labels is that they tend to complicate something which is very simple. They turn what is basic to human nature into a rarefied -ism or -ology. So while we use labels like "integrated learning" or "whole language," we should be aware that we are not talking about a new method of "teaching" children. We are talking about the ways in which we meet the age-old learning needs of the child. Intuitively, we know what those needs are, but it does help us to have them spelled out in clear terms by the results of current research into brain learning. Let us look at some of the principles that govern the way we learn.

We know that the search for meaning is basic to the human brain. It is compulsory, part of our instinct for survival. We must make sense of our experience. From this learning, we act on our environment.

The child's need to make meaning of her experience is obsessive and tireless. We sometimes say that learning is second nature to a child. It is not. It is first nature, attached to the primal survival instinct. To exist on this planet, the young child must learn about his environment and learn quickly. What we see in effect is a child driven by curiosity.

I was told a charming story about a mother with a two-month-old baby who went to a friend's house for lunch. After a meal consisting in part of sausages, the mother sat in a comfortable chair to feed her infant. The three-year-old of the house had never seen a baby being breast-fed before. He asked a number of questions, which the baby's mother answered as best she could. Then came the big question: "Where does the milk come from?"

The young woman did her best. "You know those sausages we had for lunch? They got all mashed up in my tummy and then they turned to milk."

The three-year-old gasped in admiration. "Oh!" he said. "Aren't sausages clever!"

He was not trying to be cute. In light of his own experience, he was putting meaning on the information he had received. We all have mental scrapbooks of similar sayings from young children.

We know that the essence of teaching is not knowledge but meaning. And because the search for meaning is irresistible, no child ever gets stuck in learning unless there is a threat of some kind. Learning is enhanced by appropriate challenge—the stimulus of the new and interesting information in a positive learning environment. And learning is inhibited by threat.

I know of only two conditions that can threaten young readers. The first is for him to be given dull and/or difficult reading material that has no meaning for him. If his early reading books do not connect with his experience of life, then he will not be able to make sense of them. The second threat, often connected to the first, is a fear of failure. A child who has known a lot of defeat will protect herself from further "failure" by shutting herself off from risk. She won't attempt anything new that could possibly threaten her. And if I can interrupt this program with an often-repeated commercial, I'll stress again the importance of all children being made to feel that they are successful achievers from the time they start school, regardless of adult evaluation of their progress.

In its search for meaning, the human brain is continuously processing the familiar and at the same time reaching out for the new. But the brain does not easily absorb isolated or fragmented information. When learning is embedded in experience, it is readily absorbed and stored in our natural memory system. This happens without effort or rehearsal. Information that is remote from experience is processed in a different way by another part of the brain, and its assimilation requires a lot of practice.

For example, suppose we see this sentence in print: "Throughout life we should learn something new every day."

We can read it once, close the book and remember it because it has meaning for us. We can relate it to our previous experience.

Now, suppose we see the same amount of print in nonsense language: "Kjpltordgp kunb lt durwfc kvbvz pratybcyh jyh wqtfg oua."

This has no meaning for us because it is outside our experience. To learn it would take some time and effort and be quite boring.

When working with emergent readers, I sometimes initiate a game that helps me discover how well they are decoding text. We pretend we live in back-to-front land where people do everything in the wrong order, such as sleeping with their feet on the pillow and having meals that begin with dessert. Then we open our book and try reading text in reverse order, beginning with the last word in a sentence instead of the first.

I ask, "What's wrong with reading that way?"

The answer is immediate. "It doesn't make sense!"

I close the book. "Can you remember the back to front sentence?"

Of course, they can't, although someone will probably give me the last two or three words.

The brain resists having meaningless patterns placed upon it, and this resistance is especially strong in young children, who don't have the learning experience to cope with isolated information. As children get older, cumulative experience will often give a background of meaning to certain fragmented information. For example, a child can make sense of word skills and drills against a solid background experience of oral and written language.

One of the criticisms leveled at natural learning is that the young reader doesn't learn word skills. Of course she does. But she learns them within the context of meaning. She begins to read the way she begins to speak, with language that has meaning and that relates to her experience. When she is familiar and comfortable with written language to the extent of feeling power over it, she will enjoy examining its parts to see how it is made. Word skills come naturally to children who know they are writers and readers. This will be dealt with in the next chapter, but here let me tell you about a visit I had to a first-grade classroom in southern California. The cultural diversity of the students could have been a challenge for the most experienced teacher. Yet here the children were not only reading and writing with confidence and enthusiasm, but also with advanced spelling skills. I asked their teacher about this.

"Oh," she said casually, "every day I say to them, 'Go and get your favorite reading book and copy out a page.' Half an hour later, I have to stop them from copying the whole book."

This method, involving a minimum of "teaching," may seem too simple to be trusted, and yet it is very effective. The children are taking responsibility for their learning and are highly motivated. They are also establishing an unconscious learning ethic. As they extend their reading skills, they automatically absorb information about language structure, which in turn influences their writing.

My early reading experience was with a phonics system that taught letters, progressing to one-syllable words, two-syllable words and so on. We then got sentences. Finally, we were trusted with reading for meaning. We got a story, but by that time many of us had come to understand that reading was a negative experience.

That brings us to the next point that has been emphasized by research: emotions are critical to learning. We don't simply learn things in an intellectual vacuum, detached from feeling. All of our learning is influenced and organized by our emotions—and our emotions are not simple either, but many-layered and interacting. Learning takes place in the entire context of what we feel about ourselves and our learning environment. For example, as you are reading this you will be affected by your physical comfort, by messages that lie outside your immediate focus, by the emotions of past experiences, by self-esteem, by personal preferences, and by the expectations you place on yourself and your reaction to the expectations of others. All of these things will be influencing the meaning my writing has for you.

We accept that learning is a complex business, unique for every individual and situation. Because each child brings a different pattern of emotions to the classroom, we can't expect any two children to learn in exactly the same way. Therefore, the more responsibility we give a child for his learning, the more effective that learning will be. The old overlay system of teacher-dictated learning was a hit-and-miss affair. It connected with some children but not with others. When the emphasis is on the child's learning rather than the teacher's teaching, the teacher can then become the midwife to an educational process that exceeds all expectations.

We know, too, that emotions facilitate the storage and recall of information. Pause here for a moment, and go back to some memory of early childhood. As you relive the details, you realize that memories are attached to feelings that are to some degree either positive or negative. In fact, all recall operates this way. Moreover, we know that the human brain has a self-protective mechanism that functions automatically if an emotion is very negative. Both the emotion and the experience attached to it are placed beyond conscious recall or are "rewritten" in our minds to save us pain.

New electronic scanning devices can actually chart the way the brain shuts down areas of activity under perceived threat. For example, a person chronically depressed shows markedly reduced brain function.

But we don't really need advanced technology to observe this phenomenon in our own lives or those of young children.

Emotions condition our receptivity to learning. Let's go back to our own school or college years and think about a subject we enjoyed and excelled in. We discover to our surprise that the pleasure and success was not due so much to our natural ability as it was to a positive learning environment. We had a good relationship with the teacher and others in the class, and we felt happy about ourselves. That influenced our attitude toward what we were learning. Years later, when that subject emerged in our conscious thinking, we felt good about it without understanding why. Therefore we tended to give this subject positive value in our lives.

We know that this can work in reverse, too. Children can learn to read and learn to hate reading at the same time if the entire reading experience is fraught with negative experience and emotion. Under some of the old reading systems, a child typically associated reading with schoolwork, study, and tests. He did not discover reading for pleasure and self-empowerment. Chances are that after he left school, he did not read another book because every time he was confronted with this possibility, all the old negative memories played in his head.

The child who has experienced learning to read as a positively exciting, creative, and empowering process, is going to project that attitude on reading for the rest of his life.

An appropriate model for the natural way we learn

to read is the way we learn to speak. In infancy, we
associate something experienced with a certain set of
sounds. The experience makes meaning of the
sounds—not the other way around. Without the
experience, the sounds are meaningless. However,
when the connection between experience and sounds is
firmly established, then the sounds have meaning as the
symbols of the experience. We hear a spoken word and
it's no longer just a noise; it has become representative
of an object or process.

When we come to reading we make a third connection: experience, sounds, and now written words.
Again, the sequence is important. Oral language
embedded in experience precedes the decoding of
printed language and gives meaning to it. We find that
children who have a background deficient in oral
language will need work in that area before they are
able to begin reading. They simply do not have the
names for things.

The parents of infants expect that their offspring will
learn to talk but don't place on them specific expectations of a certain number of words by a specific date.
Nor do they introduce their child to spoken language by
presenting meaningless segments of language: "C-a-t, r-
a-t, b-a-t, m-a-t." When the child approximates
language he is greeted with delight and praise. No one
reproaches him for getting a word wrong. It is recog-
nized that each child will learn to speak differently, and
children are not compared with each other. Systems of
regular testing are not imposed. Parents will monitor a
child's progress, and if a three-year-old has a speech

problem they will probably recognize that specialized help is needed. But the large majority of children become fluent speakers through natural learning with modeling coming from adults and their peers. Any formal "teaching" is likely to inhibit rather than encourage progress.

When the child is well on her way to being a confident and fluent speaker, she will move into a new phase of language. Words have given meaning to her experience; now she wants to give meaning to her experience of language. Why do words sound the way they do? What makes them sound like other words? Why do some words make a noise like the thing they represent? Some words have quiet sounds. Some have scratchy sounds. Some words are little and some words are big.

The child becomes fascinated with the components of language and begins to experiment with onomatopoeic sound, rhymes, puns, word jokes, and the like. She makes up new sounds, plays games with words, and begins to use language as a tool for creation.

If the child does not have adequate language models, if he is verbally abused or threatened by adult expectations, if his curiosity goes unanswered or is repressed, he will suffer oral language deficiency.

We must recognize the crucial importance of creating rich and safe learning environments for children who are making the language extension from oral to printed and written words. Early reading and writing is for meaning. It accesses story. And every classroom is rich in story—pictorial, oral, and written. The pictures in early reading books are captioned by familiar spoken words that have certain shapes when printed. As the print becomes familiar, children go into the second stage of development and begin experimentation. They want to know about sentence construction, about word families and word function, how groups of letters represent certain sounds, and why some letters have no sound at all. Against the background of confident and fluent reading and writing, language skills develop naturally. The child's interest in the structure of written language is used by an enthusiastic teacher to encourage the child to take responsibility for language research and to use his discovery in creative writing.

To the child who knows she is a successful reader and writer, language skill exercises have meaning.

Chapter Five

Story in the Classroom

*T*here are many text resources that deal with language in the elementary school classroom and the development of reading and writing strategies. That is not the function of this book, but we will look at the ways we meet the child's two-way need for story. By two-way, I mean the need to *learn* and the need to *create* from that learning.

Usually, young children have two ways of creating stories even before they begin reading. They create stories by talking and by drawing pictures. That blob of red paint surrounded by slashes of purple and green may mean little to the observer, but to the artist it is a story. Invite any young child to tell you about his painting. You won't hear how he painted it, what paint he used, or the title of the work. You will hear a story: "This is Father Christmas and he got stuck in the chimney and some mans got a hammer and they bash-bashed the chimney down" (from Aaron, age 5). "This is a spider what gobbles up peoples. He gobbled up all the peoples on TV and the kids watched a video" (from Drew, age 5).

In a story-rich classroom, the teacher uses every opportunity to convert the child's pictorial/oral story to print. To an outsider, the class looks like an art gallery of startling color and energy. Examples of teacher-printed story are everywhere. "Debbie's cat is Ginger, and it hides in the laundry basket." "Marveen saw a frog as big as a house." "There was a party for Juanita's little sister." "John hates to eat olives." "Whales sing songs to their babies." "Tony's dad tried to put on Tony's T-shirt." And so on.

In the whole learning classroom, the child's own story is both part and product of the search for meaning.

What about reading texts in the story-rich classroom? They, too, need to be high-interest, child-centered stories presented in pictures and language that are within the child's experience.

Emergent readers will experience story books in several ways. One of their first reading experiences will be with a group directed by the teacher or another student reading a Big Book. They will also be assisted and encouraged to read on their own from smaller story books that have texts so simple that success is guaranteed. And they will have buddy reading, the sharing of a book with another student.

Whatever the book experience and whatever the teaching strategy, it is important that the pleasure of story is enhanced, not diminished. How many of us would be enthusiastic about reading a book if we knew that the experience was to be followed by word study lists and comprehension tests? In the whole learning classroom, testing needs to go underground. It must become a discreet monitoring that does not intrude on the child's natural rate of learning. Nor does it ever threaten the child by creating in her an awareness of the possibility of failure.

Now that we have discussed the content of early reading books, let's deal with their structure. I've said that books should be love-based. They should affirm and support the child. They should have integrity and be true to the child's world, with a real story and a satisfying ending. They should meet the child's expectations of learning to read by containing simple text.

Here are some other considerations:

1. **Size and shape.** A book should be "friendly," not so big that the child can't comfortably possess it, and not so small that it doesn't feel like a real book.

2. **Cover.** These must be attractive and appealing to the touch as well as the eye. Children have more physical contact with books than do adults. They hug them, smell them, rub their faces against them, and sleep with them. I've seen children licking the covers of their books. The appearance of a book needs to account for the close relationship a child will have with it.

   The cover illustration gives meaning to the title and tells the young reader what the book is about. Depending on how it is directed by the title, the cover illustration can lead into the story, but generally it should not give away the ending of the story.

3. **Illustrations.** Again, these should be child-centered, active, interesting, and without adult sentimentality. It is good for children to experience visual story in a variety of media: watercolors, dyes, oils, crayons, pastels, woodcuts, and collage, just as they themselves are encouraged to experiment in these media.

   Young children enjoy cartoon characters in book illustrations, but they feel threatened by excessive distortion. Great exaggeration in drawing, especially of figures, is frightening.

   Similarly, children need a lot of eye contact in their pictures. They feel uncomfortable with books in which characters' faces are not seen—e.g., back or three-quarters back views.

   In early emergent material, the artist must illustrate for meaning—no more, no less. Extraneous material in the illustrations will confuse the young reader who is looking to the picture to provide reading cues.

   The illustrations need to follow word order. If the text refers to a cat and a dog, the illustration should show a cat and a dog, not a dog and a cat.

   Left to right sequencing is important. Action shown and meaning conveyed by the illustrations should move from left to right to facilitate the flow of the story and correct page handling. Show a character moving from right to left, and chances are that a child will turn the page backwards to see where the character is going.

4. **Text.** There should be a real story with repetition and a high degree of predictability. Much of the story is

revealed through the pictures, but the text should have meaning and story shape. The textual changes must be gradual and easily managed. The story should also have a satisfying conclusion.

The story should lend itself to innovation so the child can exercise his own creative efforts. Children who yet lack the skills to structure written language in a satisfying way, can use the basic structure of a book's text for their own story ideas.

The Big Book for Shared Reading

Most of the above criteria apply also to oversize enlarged-print books used for shared reading, commonly known as Big Books. But because Big Books are designed for group reading, the language in them is developed for chant.

Big Books should have rhythmical stories told in interesting language that can be effectively used by groups of children. The individual reader might feel a little self-conscious about using dramatic language, but in the group she is offered the security of her peers. Rhyme, alliteration, changes in volume (represented by varying the size of the print), singing, and sound effects—any of these can enhance the enjoyment of shared reading.

Big Books should not have too much text. Some publishers work on the theory that because the page is big it can accommodate a lot of text. That is *not* what Big Books are about. At the early emergent level, one to four lines of text is adequate. Even at more advanced levels, eight lines is about maximum.

In Big Books, as in individual reading books, the illustrations must support the text. To test this we can simply put our hands over the text and try to read the meaning of the story from the pictures. If we can't do this, the illustrations are inadequate.

The effective Big Book is a good model for classroom innovation. Using the model of language structure and picture sequence, classes can make their own Big Books by substituting their own text, illustrations, characters, and situations.

Chapter Six

The Child as Author and Artist

W hen working with children, our starting point is always the authority and dignity of the child's world.

How much authority does the child have? If we look at our communications media, we see that the message underlying all adult words and actions is that big people have all the power. The little person is important in that one day he or she will be a big person. Generally, children are seen as adult investment. They don't have status of their own.

In recognizing the child's authority, however, we validate the child within us. We need to remind ourselves that our own childhood is not something we've put behind us. We carry it with us and we need to keep in touch with it if we are to give children the dignity, respect, and understanding that is their due.

The world of childhood is richly imaginative and hugely creative. It is a "story" world. In the same day, a four-year-old draws shapes with chalk on the shed

wall, has a telephone conversation with an imaginary
friend, dresses up as a mother going to town with
twenty children, makes a clay monster that eats cars,
paints a picture of herself (very big) and her younger
brother (very small), and hides a book with a scary
picture in it at the bottom of the drawer. All of these
activities are a part of her normal story world that is
always active, always working to make meaning of her
place in her environment. And there is something else
we should remind ourselves of: for the young child,
stories are vehicles for feeling. Stories offer symbols
that make meaning out of chaos. Stories siphon off
emotional energy, making that energy creative. As
children get older and expand their story-making skills,
story also means exploration of language, the manipula-
tion of an audience, and the means of relating
information. But to the young story maker, story is
primarily an expression of feeling.

Of course the arts are cathartic for adults too, but this
is especially so for the child, who does not have the
experience of life or the skill to name what he is feeling
and why.

And there is something else we need to remember:
children have adult-sized emotions. Maybe they are
organized in a different way, but they have the same
intensity. Can you remember back to a time in childhood when you had inside you a storm that threatened
to blow you apart? What did you do? How did adults
react?

At the age of two and a half, the child is vigorously
claiming independence from his parent. He wants to do

everything for himself, and at this stage the parent has the task of discerning between freedom and license. The child needs space in which to learn, but at the same time boundaries are set for his safety. At two and a half years old, ritual becomes important. Look at the way a toddler ritualizes eating, lining up peas on a plate, digging wells in mashed potatoes, eating separately the layers of a hamburger, nibbling precise holes in a slice of bread. Meals offer a lot of opportunity for story.

I watched a three-year-old making an island of her breakfast oatmeal. Her commentary went something like this: "I'm eating the trees and I'm eating the houses and I'm eating the people and I'm eating the shops." (Even her language was ritualized.) Eventually the oatmeal was gone and she pushed away a bowl about one-third filled with milk.

I said, "What about the sea?"

She gave me a stern look. "Sharks!"

By three, the child's world is richly furnished with story. At this stage parents usually help children to make a distinction between fact and fantasy. It's important that children learn such a distinction, but at the same time, fact should not be valued over fantasy. Made-up stories are wonderful treasures, the symbols of the child's inner world, and they should never be dismissed as trivial.

Some parents can become concerned about two aspects of children's story. The first is what adults may call "the telling of lies." Now "telling lies" is an adult concept. The child is using his experience of language to describe a feeling that is too strong for a factual account. If the child is in the habit of telling stories to avoid the consequences of certain actions, then the motivating feeling is probably fear, and it's time for the parent to look at his or her communication with the child concerning these actions.

The other common concern among parents is the amount of violence that surfaces in children's story. I know this alarms teachers, too. Often the problem lies in our not realizing that violence in a child's story means different things for the child than it does for the adult. As adults, we see violence as antisocial and threatening behavior. Children, however, experience violence in a story differently. For the child, the violent story is the expression of a highly charged emotional state. If release is not found in story, it can erupt as violent physical behavior or else turn inward to lay the groundwork for later emotional problems.

As I mentioned before, I do not sanction strong expressions of violence in children's story. And as teachers and parents, we must always be increasing the child's awareness of options to violence. But we must also look at what is happening in the child's life and see her emotions as valid. We must respect what the child is feeling.

When telling stories, young children will draw symbolic characters from their language experience, using characters from story books or television. I believe that the degree of violence is not due so much to indoctrination from these books, comics, or TV programs as it is to the intensity of the child's emotional state. Thus a six-year-old girl's story about a witch who killed a baby princess is more likely to be about sibling rivalry than old fairy tales. Children simply borrow characters to make their feelings visible.

Another obvious reminder is that the subtext of all children's story is autobiographical. We can ban and burn all violent books and films, but we are not going to change the child's need to release his emotional state in the form of story.

In the 1960s, Sylvia Ashton-Warner described young children as volcanoes with twin vents—block the creative vent, she said, and the destructive one will blow.

Children's Stories

We all know what happens to a child when the creative vent is blocked. But here let me share with you some work from children who have made meaning of their lives through story. These children, six to eight years old, were considered to have special needs. They were in a creative writing workshop in which I had asked them to take on a nonhuman identity. After a time of discussion, they wrote the following stories. (I have corrected spelling but not punctuation, preferring to leave the original rhythm of the stories intact.)

This first story is from a seven-year-old girl who was in the middle of a large, closely controlled family.

Scaredy Cat

Scaredy Cat he's a married cat he's married to a bossy cat and scaredy cat he is scared of rats and rats are sometimes scared of Scaredy cat and scaredy cat he's scared of mice. Mice treat him like a slave. And rats treat him like slaves. They tell him to get cheese or else they will kill him.

Another seven-year-old girl chose to be a pear. Here is her story.

Pearl Pear

I was sitting on a tree when someone said you're in trouble Pearl Pear. Why? I asked. Because someone is going to eat you. Who said that? I asked. I looked up and saw a bird a giant bird that chased me down the tree.

And here he comes. Ha! ha! ha! said the bird. The boy picked me up and was going to take a bite but I bit his nose. The boy cried. I laughed at the boy. The bird flew down and pecked me. I was so sore I screamed out but in the end I was all right and the bird was hurt.

If we examine the subtext of these stories we find that a common theme is coping with powerlessness. It occurs again in this story written by an eight-year-old girl.

The Six Inches Tall Man That Can Do Judo

I am a very small man who is six inches tall. One day I went to town and I saw something up in the sky. It looked like some cotton wool. But then I looked up and saw a big big giant. The big big giant said to another giant, Look at that tiny tiny kind of an ant! Well that is what the giant said. Anyway I said, Oh

no, I will have to show him what I can do. I might
just have to do judo on them. Oh! Ah! Oh! Oh! Great!
I yelled when they were flat on the ground. That got
rid of them. All of a sudden this dust came out of
their hands and I grew to the proper size.

The following story came from an eight-year-old boy.

The Two Countries
Once upon a time Australia and New Zealand got
married and they had a lot of children and they
turned into islands. One day an Aborigine
camped by Australia and he speared Australia.
Australia died and New Zealand and the islands
had a sad party and lived.

I later learned that this boy's parents had separated.
His father had gone to Australia, and the family hadn't
heard from him for two years.

Here is a story from an autistic ten-year-old girl who
had severe communication difficulties. This was her
first written story.

Snappy
My wish is to be a pair of scissors, He wanted to cut
me up. I was sad. I nipped his finger. He screamed
to the teacher, he hit me because he hates me! Why
did you kick me I asked. Because you wanted me to
do it, said the boy. He said, you stupid scissors you
don't cut properly. I felt sadder. He changed to
number 20 and it cut up cardboard. They were like
snips. You're my best friend I said to number 20 and

we loved each other so number 20 showed me tricks
and I cut silver card.

The subtext of this story is extraordinary. Remember
that this young author had not written a story before.
She was disruptive in class. Her habit of kicking, biting,
and scratching meant that she often had to be physically
restrained or removed from the room. In the "story-
talk" period before writing, she became excited,
shouting out that she was going to become scissors and
cut people up, and the beginning of the story does
reveal her anguish. But the act of communicating this
pain, of actually doing something with it, had a
markedly liberating effect on her. We can see the
movement from powerlessness to empowerment as this
young author discovers her authority. She makes
friends with herself. She uses the beautiful image of
cutting up silver card. Like so much of the violent
writing that comes from children, this is a story of
healing.

Indeed, all of these examples with the exception of
the first have a similar upbeat ending. I see the first
writing as unfinished. Perhaps the young author ran
out of time. Her story *Scaredy Cat* has only two parts, a
beginning and a middle. Each of the other stories have
three: the introduction, the problem, and the solution to
the problem. Young children want to read stories with
this classic beginning, middle, and ending structure,
and in their own stories they seem to use it as a
problem-solving device.

We come back to Sylvia Ashton-Warner's image of
the child as a volcano with twin vents, and we give

ourselves another simple and obvious reminder: when we increase creativity in the classroom, we diminish antisocial behavior.

As I travel in the United States visiting schools, I see wonderful acts of creation everywhere, young volcanoes spouting story, and classrooms full of eager authors and artists. As soon as I walk into a class, I know what is happening. The place is humming like a beehive, and walls are covered with children's creative works—not adult posters but stories, paintings, projects, and poems authored by children. These schools are a graphic example of our last reminder: when we give children authority we don't get chaos, we get art. We get authors. We get poets. We get young people fully alive to learning.

In one very creative California school in which I spent some time was a special needs class, where all the students knew without a doubt that they were accomplished authors and illustrators. An eleven-year-old boy with Down's syndrome had just published a book and wanted me to read it. Here it is:

The Gun-Eater

The gun-eater came down to earth. He saw all the graves. He saw all the sad people. He was sad. Then the gun-eater ate all the guns in the world and there were no more guns. The end.

The young author asked me, "Do you like my story?" I told him I thought it was the most important story I'd ever read.

Here again are those points that we know and need to keep remembering:

1. When working with children, our starting point is always the authority and dignity of the child's world.
2. Our own childhood is not behind us but within us.
3. For the young child, stories are vehicles for feeling.
4. The young child has adult-sized emotions.
5. The violent story is the expression of a highly charged emotional state that needs release.
6. The subtext of all story is autobiographical.
7. When we increase creativity in the classroom we diminish antisocial behavior.
8. When we give children authority we don't get chaos, we get art. We get children alive to education.

As I said at the beginning, none of this is new. It has all been written before, if not on paper, then in the truth of our own hearts. The needs of the child do not change with the generations, and the challenges and expectations that children bring with them into the classroom today are the same as they have always been. Today's child may not have a background shaped by slavery, famine, or the horrors of war, but there are other forms of imprisonment, hunger, and violence. The outer trappings of the cause change; the effect remains the same; and on the whole, society tends to be no better or worse today than in our great-grandparents' time. In my observations, the most successful teachers are the ones who work not from a center of academic training but from the child within them. I do not diminish the value of qualifications. Teacher education is necessary and important, and it provides the tools that are used in the classroom. But how these tools are employed comes back to a teacher's appreciation of his or her own childhood needs and the ability to meet those needs in the students—the need for security, the need for stimulating challenge, and, above all, the need for appreciation.

An Open Letter to Teachers

Dear Teacher,

It may seem a little unusual to end a book with a letter,
but it is an appropriate response to the thousands of
letters I have received from American teachers. Because
a letter can be informal and personal I can say in it
things that are important but do not have a place in the
body of the book.

The most important is a heartfelt request: believe in
yourselves. American kindergarten and grade school
teachers are the best qualified in the world, and yet they
tend to get poor press in their own country. I don't
know why this is so. All I can say is that in my ten-year
relationship with The Wright Group I have had associa-
tions with thousands of schools, thousands of teachers,
and literally millions of children in all parts of the
country. Over the years my respect for American
teachers has grown into huge admiration. Here are
some of the attributes I have observed:

American teachers work incredibly hard. I don't

know of any other profession where people devote so much of their own time to unpaid work in preparation for classes, personal concern for pupils, and acquisition of further teaching skills. Pursuit of excellence seems to be the prime motivation of the teaching profession. There is little evidence of complacency. I see everywhere the strong desire to do everything well.

The American spirit of democracy is established in the classroom. Children are encouraged at an early age to make decisions and take responsibility for their learning. The teacher, like a wise president, knows the value of diplomacy and works on the old adage that "you can catch more flies with a teaspoon of honey than a gallon of vinegar."

The national characteristic of friendliness also has its beginnings in the elementary classrooms. Visitors are impressed by the courtesy and spontaneity young people offer not only them and their teacher but also each other. There is an atmosphere of caring and sharing and open communication that will foster social responsibility in later years.

Generally, American teachers have the greatest gift any teacher can offer students—enthusiasm. Working on the sound principle that the most effective learning is "caught" rather than "taught," they share with their pupils their own delight in knowledge, their own love of reading, their own pride in achievement. This upbeat approach to teaching with its accompanying messages of love, laughter, and affirmation is the best. It reinforces for me the awareness that teaching is first and foremost about feelings.

So thank you, dear teacher, for all the knowledge and love you are investing in future generations. Like Atlas, you carry the world on your shoulders, and at times you will be aware of the weight. But don't allow an occasional negative response to damage your faith in yourself.

You are a remarkable person doing the greatest job on this earth.

With love and gratitude,

Joy Cowley